Purpose

Discover and Fulfill Your Life Purpose

Nolen Rollins

Published by Kingdom Mobilization Press, June 28, 2014, Estero, Florida, USA

REVISED by Kingdom Mobilization Press, April 15, 2015, Estero, Florida, USA
Kingdom Mobilization, Inc.
20041 South Tamiami Trail, Suite 1
Estero, Florida, USA, 33928
www.kingmo.org

Purpose
Discover and Fulfill Your
Life Purpose
Table of Contents

Purpose: Discover and Fulfill Your Life Purpose

This book is dedicated to my life purpose coaches ...

Dr. Henry Blackaby who has been providentially there for me for over 25 years as a spiritual mentor, especially in the transitional stages of my life

Bob Buford, Founder of the Halftime Movement, who has been my greatest encourager to pursue helping others to discover and fulfill their life purposes

Introduction …
You Were Created by God to Make a Difference in the World

You Are Special!

Yes, you are special and you are unique. There is no one else on earth just like you. You may be thinking, "Why, you don't even know me. How can you say that you believe I am special?"

I know that you are special without any doubt. God made you special. I know God made you special because I believe God's Word is true. The Psalmist declared, "I praise you (God), for I am fearfully and wonderfully made (by You). Wonderful are your works; my soul knows it very well." (Psalm 139:14, parentheses mine) You are a wonderful creation of God. Know it well.

You Have a Purpose Here on Earth

Again, you may question, "How can you know that God has a purpose for my life? There are some days that I feel like my life is purposeless or even wasted."

And once again, I can state with confidence that I know God has a special plan for your life because He tells us so in His Word. "For I know the plans I have for you, declares the Lord, plans for welfare and not for evil, to give you a future and a hope." (Jeremiah 29:11) God has a plan and purpose for your life to give you a blessed hope for a meaningful future.

You Can Make a Difference in the World

God wants you to make a difference in the world. He created you with particular skills, abilities, passions, personality, strengths and gifts and has given you specific life experiences for a reason - so that you may successfully fulfill your God-given purpose here on earth.

Refuse to live your life without a sense of purpose. Refuse to go through life without knowing God's special plan and purpose for you. Refuse to come to the end of your life and wonder if your life really mattered.

Discover and fulfill your God-given purpose. Understand how God designed you with special abilities and how to maximize them. Leave a legacy of impact in the lives of others. Make a difference in the world. Have a strong sense of significance as well as success in life. Do what God created you to do here on earth. Be a world-changer!

The Purpose for this Book on Purpose

After having a very successful ministry for over thirty years, I became somewhat disillusioned because most people I knew were not living as people who knew their purposes. They may have been living good lives, but they had little or no sense of significance.

This is true for people in different stages of life. Many college graduates complete their formal education only to feel confusion about what's next. Young parents often desire more in life than just paying the price to pursue the American dream. Mid-career professionals wonder if the path they have chosen will bring meaning to their lives. Older adults are asking, "Is this all there is?"

This was expressed well by a friend of mine who stated, "I have been successful by the world's standards, but I feel no success in my heart. I do not know that my life is making any real difference." He was not an exception; he was the norm.

In 2003 I began a long journey of seeking to discover how to solve this critical problem. I knew that God had put each of us here on earth for a reason but did not know how to help people live their lives "on purpose." I felt "called by God" to pursue my purpose of helping others discover and fulfill their purposes.

I am deeply grateful for renowned author, Rick Warren, for his best selling masterpiece, **The Purpose Driven Life**. Rick Warren helped millions of people understand that God has a purpose for their lives.

And that brings us to the reason for this additional book on purpose. Over the past ten years, I have developed a process to help individuals not only know that God has a purpose for them but will also help them discover and fulfill their God-given purposes in life. It is my passion and desire that this book will encourage you to take the journey to discover and engage in your purpose.

This process is called the **GPS Life Journey**. GPS stands for "God's Plan for Significance" and implies that there is direction from above for your journey in life. The **GPS Life Journey** answers three life-changing questions ...

- Who am I? How did God design me? How can I know myself?

- How do I hear from God and get His plan and purpose for my life?

- What is God's purpose for the next stage of my life? Why did God put me here on earth?

As you learn about the **GPS Life Journey**, my prayer is that you will realize that ...

- You are special.

- You have a special purpose here on earth.

- You can make a difference in the world.

- You can live a life of significance.

This is an interactive book. You can choose to read it through quickly. I recommend that you read it with pen in hand and take time to reflect. Answer the questions and give responses as indicated. This way you will get maximum benefit from your reading of the book. Now, Bon Voyage, as you seek God's Plan for Significance for your life!

God's Plan
for Success
by Nolen Rollins

I know the plans I have for you,
Declares the Lord, and this is true;
Not plans for harm nor for distress,
But for your good and for success.

God has an ordained purpose for you,
You are destined to see it through;
Are you aware of His mission,
Can you see His clear vision?

You are gifted, you are unique,
And His purpose you need to seek;
Fulfill His plan, your destiny,
And change the world, your legacy.

Most never ask, they never know,
They never search, and do not grow;
Just struggle through their busy life,
Do what they must, deal with the strife.

But not you, my friend, you must soar,
Pursue God's best, He has far more;
Discover purpose, know His plan;
Fulfill your mission, yes, you can!

One

God Has a Purpose and Plan for You

You Can Know and Fulfill God's Purpose for Your Life Here on Earth

God has a purpose and plan for everyone here on earth. Yet most people never fulfill that purpose because they have never asked the question, "What is God's purpose and plan for my life?" We all want to be successful and live a life of significance. We desire to make a difference in the world, at least in that part of the world where we do life and have the opportunity to impact the lives of others. You can know God's plan for your life. God wants you to know His purpose for you and for you to fulfill that purpose.

What Is Success?

How do you define success? Everyone wants to be successful. No one wants to be a failure. God has a plan for success for your life and you can discover His plan. Unfortunately, success is largely defined by Hollywood, Madison Avenue and Wall Street. We are constantly bombarded in the media by false images of what success should look like. When easily accessible TV comes to a region of the world, consumerism increases many times over, even in impoverished countries of the world. We don't know we need what we need until the media tells us we need it!

Many people define success in ways that may not be God's plan for their success.

- Position – being a person of high rank and importance
- Prestige – being famous, a person that others admire
- Power – being a person of great power and influence
- Possessions – having all the fine luxuries of life

Many people have pursued these definitions of success only to become terrible failures.

The basic premise of this book is simple, yet missed by the vast majority of individuals in the world. **God's plan for success and significance in your life is to discover your purpose for being here on earth and fulfill that purpose.**

A recent graduate of nearby Florida Gulf Coast University approached me about participating in a **GPS Life Journey** small group I was about to begin. Typically, the kind of individuals who have been most interested in the **GPS Life Journey** have been older and are approaching the end of their professional careers.

So I asked Robert with considerable curiosity, "Why are you interested in the GPS process?" His candid response alerted me to the fact that the **GPS Life Journey** is for anyone. Robert replied, "I have watched my Christian parents pursue the fabled American dream only to wake up from a nightmare of worldly success and broken relationships. I do not want to follow that path. I want to take the journey to God's success for my life."

God Has a Plan for You

God has a plan for your life. May I refer you again to the Prophet Jeremiah. "For I know the plans I have for you, declares the Lord, plans for welfare and not for evil, to give you a future and a hope." (Jeremiah 29:11)

This word of hope came to the people of God in the midst of their darkest hour – during Babylonian captivity after the destruction of their homes and homeland. Even though you may be in the midst of difficulty, God has a plan for you that is good; it will give you a future and hope.

Notice at least four very important facts in this scripture.

- God has a plan for you.
- God knows His plan for you.
- God's plan is for your good, not to harm you.
- God's plan for you is to give you hope and a future.

God knows His plan and purpose for your life. Do you? If you do not, I have good news. You can know His purpose for your life. You cannot invent His purpose. You cannot dream up His purpose. You can only discover His purpose as he reveals it to you. He is not deliberately trying to make it difficult for you to discover your purpose. God not only knows His purpose for your life, He wants you to know your purpose and to be actively engaged in fulfilling it. As a matter of fact, that is why He put you here on earth!

God Had a Plan for You before You Were Born

I believe that God has a special purpose for each of us for which we have been uniquely equipped. We learn this in the Bible in the Apostle Paul's letter to the Ephesians. Most followers of Jesus Christ are familiar with Ephesians 2:8-9, where Paul declares we receive the salvation of God by grace through faith. Yet most followers of Christ are not familiar with Ephesians 2:10, which tells us, "For we are his workmanship, created in Christ Jesus for good works, **which God prepared beforehand,** that we should walk in them." You were created to carry out these good works that God prepared for you, even before you were born!

You are special. God uniquely shaped you for a special purpose – His purpose for your life.

No one is here on earth by accident. Each of us is placed on earth by the providence of an Almighty God, who creates and sustains everyone and everything.

"Well, I'm not so sure I can buy into that," you may be thinking.

"If God has a purpose for my life, why do I often have a sense of emptiness and meaninglessness?"

Maybe it is because you, like the vast majority of other individuals in the world, have not discovered God's special purpose for your life. Significance comes from fulfilling God's will and His plan for your life.

Some people try to find a sense of significance and fulfillment in doing everything. They volunteer for every opportunity and say yes to every request for service. Sadly, they not only still feel unfulfilled, they also feel very tired.

Popular author Henry Blackaby states, "Most Christians are so busy doing the work of the church that they miss the will of God!" That is not to say that church work might not be God's plan for your life. It is saying that doing everything is not God's will for your life. The key to success is not doing all you can but doing what God specifically designed you to do.

God does have a purpose for your life. He has good works that he designed just for you to do even before you were born. His good works for you are not to do as much as you can but to fulfill His plan. This is God's plan for success and significance for your life.

God Has General Purposes for Everyone

There are some things according to scripture that are God's plan for everyone. For example, God desires that everyone should repent and follow Jesus, obey the commands of His Word, and serve others.

II Peter 3:9, "The Lord is not slow to fulfill his promise as some count slowness, but is patient toward you, not wishing that any should perish, but that **all should come to repentance.**"

Deuteronomy 4:2, "You shall not add to the word that I command you, nor take from it, that you may **keep the commandments of the Lord your God** that I command you."

I Peter 4:10, "As each has received a gift, use it to **serve one another**, as good stewards of God's varied grace."

Every follower of Jesus Christ should seek to fulfill God's general purposes for everyone.

God Has a Specific Purpose for You

God has a plan for each of us to bring Him glory while we are here on earth. Certainly fulfilling this purpose includes His general purposes for everyone. But God does not desire that we should do everything. Jesus Christ, while here on earth, did not attempt to do everything. He did not go around performing every good work that could be done. He did not heal all the sick, feed all those who were hungry or raise all the dead. He did only what the Father showed Him to do. God the Father put Jesus Christ the Son here on earth for a specific purpose.

"The Son can do nothing of his own accord, but only what he sees the Father doing. For whatever the Father does, that the Son does likewise." (John 5:19) God had specific good works for the Son to do while He was here on earth. Jesus knew and fulfilled God the Father's purpose for His life.

Neither does God intend for you to do every good work you can while here on earth. That leads to burnout. God desires that you do the good works that He planned beforehand especially for you.

Glory to God in the Highest!

By fulfilling God's purpose for his coming to earth, Jesus brought glory to God the Father. In Jesus' conversation with His Father just before going to the cross to pay the sin debt of the entire world, He reported that He had brought glory to God. "I glorified you on earth, **having accomplished the work that you gave me to do**." (John 17:4)

Jesus knew the Father's purpose for Him while He was here on earth. He was fully committed to carrying out that mission. By doing so, He accomplished God's purpose for His coming to earth and thereby brought glory to God. If Jesus Christ brought glory to God the Father while here on earth by accomplishing the work that God gave Him to do, you too will bring glory to God by discovering and fulfilling His specific purpose for you while you are here on earth.

GPS Life Journey Story ...
Change the Way You Think!
by Risa Baker

I have been a Christian most of my life and I have struggled with being, doing, impatience, finishing one thing and ready to move on to the next - always striving for something more and wondering does God have a plan for me? Am I doing it? It always seemed to be just out of my reach. I just couldn't get the clarity I needed - clarity of gifts and skills, clarity of purpose, clarity of dreams and passions.

Everyone wants more of something - more happiness, more passion, more success. Could I really have more clarity? Was there a secret to living a fulfilled life, to knowing what I love and being able to do it?

Then I discovered the **GPS Life Journey** which enabled me to discover that I love coaching and working with people, motivating them to find their unique mission and impact the world. Really!

I discovered that I am gifted, experienced and skilled in doing this very thing. Imagine that! This was no surprise to God, but it sure was to me. I was so excited about this discovery that I have felt compelled to share this amazing opportunity with family, friends and literally people all around the globe. At last,

21

a God-given passion, an epiphany - not just a game-changer, but a life-changer!

"Risa, I just have to tell you that last week I had my very first Bible study ever with some women. It is because of your willingness to allow God to use you to change lives! I am so excited for this endeavor. I felt anointed and felt such confirmation that God has this for me. I am so excited to see what God will do with this group and I wanted to share this with you. What you are doing is making a difference!"

Romans 12:2 says, "… but let God transform you into a new person **by changing the way you think.** Then you will learn to know God's will for you, which is good and pleasing and perfect." (New Living Translation)

Take the challenge. Change the way you think. You can serve and change lives and have fun doing it. Refuse the status quo. Impact lives. Make a difference. You can **know** and **do** what God created you to do.

Risa Baker is a certified **GPS Life Journey** Facilitator and Life Purpose Coach for facilitation of transformation, an author, speaker, wife, mother, grandmother, and people-lover. She may be contacted at risa@risabaker.com.

Two

Mission Unknown

Few Are On Mission

T he vast majority of people in this world never discover and engage in their God-designed purposes. It is not that they face "mission impossible," they simply have no clue about what their missions are. You cannot be on mission if you do not clearly understand what your mission is.

It has been my privilege to serve as a consultant and leadership trainer in a variety of venues. I have helped facilitate training for churches of all sizes, other non-profit organizations, denominational conferences, Christian school leadership conventions and for-profit businesses. While the vast majority of my experience has been in mega-church leadership, I feel like I have a fairly accurate view of what's going on in many types of organizations of all sizes.

I have discovered one discouraging, common thread that runs through most of these organizations. The vast majority of individuals never discover and engage in fulfilling God's purposes for their lives.

I have consistently surveyed leaders about personal mission for over 30 years. When I ask, "How many of you can stand up right now and clearly state your personal mission statement?" less than 2% of Christian leaders in ministry or in business ever respond positively. Most of those who do respond are quoting a corporate mission statement for which they have little passion and commitment.

Not only do leaders not have a personal mission statement, they have never even given the subject a passing thought. If this is true of leaders, how much more true is it for followers?

Let's test my theory. Do you know your personal God-given mission? Can you state it instantly and clearly without having to go find it written somewhere in the archives? Does it drive your life behavior and your daily decision making? Are you passionate about it?

Little Standards Lead to Little Success

I am afraid that Christian leaders have unintentionally given people in our organizations a weak standard for Christian living. By where we place our priority focus we have led people to believe that the essence of living the Christian life is faithful attendance in our organizations, serving in some volunteer capacity and giving to support the work of our organizations. Of course there is nothing wrong with these activities. The problem is people believing that this is all there is to living a life of success and significance. By setting our standards so low, we have led people to be satisfied with busyness rather than being fulfilled in following God's plan for their lives.

Bob was my Job (Old Testament character Job). I would gladly have held him up to all others and proclaimed. "Have you considered my servant Bob?" Bob did everything. He was incredible! He taught Sunday School, served as a deacon, tithed (That alone made him a saint in my book.), shared his faith, sung in the choir, and volunteered for many special projects.

I was shocked when he solemnly approached me with a look of doom and gloom and said, "We have to talk." Comfortably seated in my office he continued, "I am not happy. I am not fulfilled. I am working as hard as I can but I still feel like God has something else, something different for me. I have no passion, other than obedience, for doing all that I am doing." As it turns out, he was not even being obedient. He was serving because of needs and not as a result of God's calling for his life.

Today I am happy to report that after Bob discovered his God-given gifts and abilities and his God-given purpose he is happily and successfully serving as the directional leader for an extremely prominent mega-church. His business background and passion for developing and encouraging leaders was what he was created for and he is loving every moment of his service for the Kingdom now.

Where Are You on Your Journey?

Let's access where you may be on your journey of finding God's plan for success for your life. Remember our definition of success - **God's plan for success and significance in your life is to discover your purpose for being here on earth and fulfill that purpose.**

Take time to do the following assessment. This assessment is not designed to make you feel guilty about where you are on your journey but to challenge you to be serious about your journey to success and significance.

Making A Difference Assessment

Please rate your present life situation in regards to the following ten statements concerning making a difference in the world.

Use a scale of 1 (low) to 5 (high) for each statement.

_____ 1. I have a significant desire for my life to make a difference in the world.

_____ 2. I have a stated personal life mission statement (not work or professional mission).

_____ 3. I can clearly, vividly describe my personal vision for the next stage of my life.

_____ 4. I have stated personal core values that drive my behavior in life.

_____ 5. I know and understand my personality type and how to function successfully in my relationships with others.

_____ 6. I understand and use my spiritual gifts in service to others.

_____ 7. I know, understand, and function within my major strengths and abilities in life.

_____ 8. I understand my greatest passions and am currently serving in ways to fulfill those passions.

_____ 9. I have determined the greatest priority action steps for making a difference in the world for the next stage of my life.

_____ 10. I am currently engaged in activities that are fulfilling my life purpose, giving me a great sense of significance, and making a difference in the world.

_____ TOTAL SCORE

How Did You Do?

Let me give you hope. Typically when individuals take this assessment before participation in the **GPS Life Journey** process, the average score is in the low to mid twenties. After completing the **GPS Life Journey,** scores range in the low to mid forties.

You do not have to go through life not knowing your mission. Remember, God has a plan for you and He knows what it is. (Jeremiah 29:11) God is not deliberately hiding His plan for your life. As a matter of fact, He strongly desires for you to know and fulfill your mission. That is what He made you for and what brings Him the greatest glory.

GPS Life Journey Story ...
Now I Know Why God
Put Me Here on Earth,
by Don Gunther

Throughout my life I have always had my own goals, but goals never tied to God. I have helped many people with career plans, but again, never thinking about what God had for me to do.

I led big projects in the billions of dollars in over 130 countries, but never thought about putting God first in my life. I thought just believing in God and attending my church were enough, but it didn't make my life meaningful.

When I moved to Naples, Florida after retirement, I realized I needed to do more than golf and fish so I got involved in non-profit work. I helped start the Naples Wine Festival and was on the board of the Gulfshore Playhouse. This helped somewhat but I still didn't feel like I was living a life of significance.

One day, through a common friend, I met Nolen Rollins, author of **GPS Life Journey**. After casual opening conversation, the first thing Nolen asked me was, "Do you know why God put you here on earth?" I told him I didn't know for sure. He then asked me if I would like to know. I said yes and that is how I got into **GPS Life Journey**. Through GPS I discovered that I should be serving and leading some effort to move others towards God.

The Immokalee Foundation, which helps migrant farm workers' children improve their education, from kindergarten through college, and then help them get a job, needed someone to serve as Chairman of the Board. I took the position and I believe, with God's help, I have made a difference.

Recently, I also helped start a local chapter of a faith-based organization called Men's Golf Fellowship. We bring men together to talk about their lives and their problems or concerns, all with the idea of helping each other.

All of this is bringing real meaning to my life and bringing me closer to Christ. Probably none of this would have been possible without the **GPS Life Journey**. Do you know why God put you here on earth?

Don Gunther and his wife, Mosey, have four children and twelve grandchildren. Don has led several organizations, including being Vice Chairman of Bechtel, chairman of a high tech company and chairman of several non-profit organizations. He is a business coach and a speaker on many business issues.

Three

Huge Untapped Potential

I Will Never Do That?

Rodger has great potential. He is a people person with amazing relational skills. Rodger also had a very successful career in the insurance business. When he retired he led the largest, most successful insurance agency in Canada.

Rodger and Donna, his equally gifted wife of many years, had been involved in serving in their church for many years. They were active in serving God. But they had never asked the question, "What is God's purpose for our lives."

When I met Rodger I realized that he had much more to offer to the Kingdom of God. He had the experiences and skills to make a greater difference in larger arenas. One day I suggested to Rodger that he should join me on one of my trips abroad to influence people in other cultures.

His response was classic, "I will never do that." I quickly cautioned him to never say never when God is listening. And we know God is always listening. Many people just need the challenge of taking a giant step forward in their service for God in His Kingdom.

Houston, We Have a Problem!

Herein lies the problem for many people in their personal experiences. People have great capacity to make a difference in their communities and the world, but rather than being engaged in such ventures for the Kingdom, they are being enlisted to hand out bulletins at door number six and serve on some dormant, ineffective committee.

How about your experience? Think about the individuals you know within your spheres of influence. Do you not see numerous individuals who have the capacity to impact the world? They are all around you. They are executives, professionals, blue-collar laborers and managers in every profession you can imagine. They have gifts, skills, experiences, abilities, strengths and passions to solve the problems of society.

Think about yourself. Do you not have passions and abilities that you feel like are not being fully utilized? Could you not make a greater difference in the Kingdom of God if you discovered your God-given mission? Do you often feel overworked and less than effective in your service? Or worse still, are you merely sitting on the sidelines watching others play the game?

The vast majority of churches and non-profit organizations do not know how to mobilize this tremendous force for the Kingdom of God. The best they can do is to persuade people to fill the multitude of slots in their "we are doing everything" programs.

The Challenge in the Kingdom of God

The challenge before us is to enlist, equip, empower and encourage these individuals to discover and engage in their God-given purposes. We can mobilize this incredible work force for the Kingdom of God. We can, we should, and we must! This is the God-given passion that drives me and many others who are serving in mobilization movements around the world.

Why? Not only for the sake of meeting the needs in the Kingdom of God, but also for the sake of people who truly desire to make a difference in the world. By the way, people really do want to do that! Do you not want to live a life of significance?

The Rest of the Story

As Paul Harvey, infamous radio commentator, would say in his beautiful baritone voice, "And now, for the rest of the story." Back to my story about my friend, Rodger. After participation in the GPS Life Journey Rodger discovered that God's purpose for his life was to use his ability to influence others to pursue God's plan and purpose for their *lives.*

It was only a few months after Rodger proclaimed, "I will never do that," that we traveled together to help others discover and engage in God's purposes for their lives in India ... and Nigeria ... and Canada.

Rodger is now on the staff of Kingdom Mobilization as the Canada Country Director. He has used his God-given abilities to fulfill his God-given mission. Thousands of individuals in Canada and all around the world are on mission because of Rodger.

Kingdom Potential Assessment

What potential do you have to change the world? Take a survey. Ask yourself these questions concerning your talents, time and treasures. You may be surprised concerning the amazing potential that God has given you … not to lie dormant, but to be utilized in His Kingdom. What capacity do you have to change the world?

Talents

What education and training do I have?

What are my artistic abilities, skills and interests?

What leadership and management skills and experiences do I have?

What trade skills and experiences do I have?

What professional skills and experiences do I have?

What ministry skills and experiences do I have?

Time

Do I have time to make a greater difference in the world?

Do I work full-time? Part-time?

Am I semi-retired?

Am I retired?

Do I have extra time in certain seasons of the year?

Am I using my time in accordance with God's priority purposes for my life?

Treasures

Do I have discretionary resources?

Do I have a giving fund? (See www.NationalChristianFoundation. org)

Am I faithfully giving at least ten percent to Kingdom causes?

How much can I and should I give to Kingdom causes?

Impressed with your God-given potential? God gave to you these talents, time and treasures to help impact the world. Be a world-changer!

GPS Life Journey Story ...
I Can Make a Difference
by Bill Myers

I have been a faithful Christian and church attendee for many years. I would consider myself a devoted follower of Jesus Christ, not perfect by any means, but committed to knowing and following Christ.

Yet I had given little thought to how I could serve Christ within my professional life other than by conducting business by the principles of the Bible. I have always had a desire to serve God and to be a faithful steward of the gifts and resources He has entrusted to me.

Then I decided to participate in a **GPS Life Journey** small group that actually met in the law office where I work. I was amazed at the clarity I received from the GPS process.

I had a clearer understanding of how God had gifted and shaped me and wanted to use me in His Kingdom. Along with that clarity came an increased passion to be used by Him.

I discovered God's mission for my life. I realized that I could carry out that mission within my normal professional responsibilities.

I was able to create both financial and time margin to serve others within my profession. I realized that I had a God-given responsibility, as part of my total life stewardship, to use my experiences and knowledge to serve God by serving others, doing what I best knew how to do.

I can make a difference in the lives of others that will have eternal Kingdom impact. How about you? Do you understand the amazing potential God has given you to make a difference in the world?

William H. Myers is a Florida Bar Board Certified Wills, Trusts and Estates Attorney. He practices estate planning, wealth preservation law and charitable gift planning with the Naples office of Porter Wright Morris and Arthur LLP where he is a partner.

Four

It Is Working All Around the World

What the World Needs Now

On April 15, 1965, Jackie DeShannan released one of my favorite songs from the glorious sixties (spoken like a true oldie). "What the world needs now is love, sweet love; it's the only thing that there's just too little of," played loudly from my tiny transistor radio. At 16 I was in love ... with every cheerleader in school.

After many years of observing Christians functioning in the Kingdom of God, I have concluded that what the world needs now is for individuals to discover and engage in their God-given missions here on earth. We have the capacity to change the world. You discovered in the last chapter that you have the tremendous potential to do so.

We can solve the problems of humanity and society. Well, actually we cannot, but God can do so through us. We can take the gospel to the world. We can feed the hungry and clothe the naked. We can provide clean water, good nutrition and medical care. We can tutor students who are failing in school and in life. We can build housing for the poor in the impoverished regions of our country and the world. We can hold the hands of cancer patients in their closing days at Hospice. We can leave our mark on a very fallen world. We can ... and we should!

Come and Listen to a Story ...

The Beverly Hillbillies was more than a popular television series to me in the sixties. It was hilarious and sad at the same time for this hillbilly who grew up in the foothills of the Smokey Mountains. It was funny to see how ridiculous people from that culture operated in the "other world." And it was sad because many of my friends growing up still think according to that culture.

That show opened up each week with the theme song, "Come and listen to the story about a man named Jed ..." I want you to listen to some brief stories of men and women who have discovered and are engaged in their God-given life purposes. These are a few of the stories of individuals who have been coached by Kingdom Mobilization or who have been through the eight-session **GPS Life Journey** process. These are the stories of people just like you who are living a life of significance and leaving a legacy.

Free-market Leadership in Former Communist Regions

In post-communist societies, people struggle in learning how to function in a free-market system. University students, who may want to know a better system, do not have access to successful free-market enterprise examples.

A small group of local businesspersons from Southwest Florida travel into the southernmost region of Russia, in the Caucasus Mountains, at least yearly to lead business and life-skills seminars. They are able help students in their preparation for success in every area of life – professional, relational, spiritual and emotional.

These professionals are doing what they do best and love doing. At their own expense they are helping others experience greater success in life. By doing so, they are experiencing a sense of significance they never before experienced.

The Power of Prayer

Retired business owner, Jerry, daily fulfills his purpose for being here on earth. His mission is to lead prayer movements for his local church, non-profit organizations, small groups, his family, and missionary friends. He is seeing the world changed through answered prayer. What greater way than prayer is there to bring about change?

Rather than only playing golf and sitting on the beach as most retired business professionals do in Florida, Jerry is leaving a legacy of significance. The answer to many of his prayers has been for him to also engage in ministry in many impoverished nations as well as in his own community.

Rescuing Individuals from Human Trafficking

Retired realtors, Lowell and Sally, established the only "safe house" in their state for caring for girls rescued from human trafficking. Their mission rescues and restores to a healthy lifestyle people from the sex trade. They minister in this arena both locally through their safe house and globally through partner organizations with similar purposes. They serve as trainers for others who desire to establish similar ministries.

When called to such a passion, their response was, "We are too old and too broke for this mission." Yet, their obedience to

God's call has had a huge impact in the lives of so many young girls. And they have never had so much fun!

Designer for Mission Projects

Sam is an young architectural designer. After participating in a **GPS Life Journey** group, he discovered that God wanted him to use his special skills as a designer to help design projects for non-profits, especially in a mission setting.

Now Sam volunteers his professional skills to help design churches, ministry centers and other facilities for mission work around the world.

Math and Science Tutor

Businessman Rich discovered his giftedness and passions prepared him to serve as a math and science tutor. Now he tutors children from his community after school several days each week. His ministry allows kids to be successful in areas where they have had serious struggles. Rich's target audience for his mission are those who cannot afford to pay a tutor.

Helping Communities Help Themselves

Bill and Sue, as full time owners and operators of senior adult services businesses, quickly discovered that not all needs in the senior adult community could be met through paid services. Consequently, at their personal expense, they founded a non-profit organization to encourage communities to take care of the needs of the people in their own communities, especially the needs of senior adults who have limited income and no local family support. Just one project of their non-profit ministry mobilizes a variety of businesses and non-profit organizations to provide Christmas gifts to thousands of needy senior adults every year. Their motto is, "Helping communities help themselves."

Giving Love and Encouragement to Kindergarteners

Jane is 85 years old. Her life is not lived in isolation. Several days a week she volunteers in local schools as a teacher's aid working with kindergarteners. Her passion is to love and encourage children who may not be receiving love and encouragement at home. Jane is helping children understand that she loves them and that God loves them too.

Discovering Purpose in Nigeria

Ken is a pastor in Nigeria, in a region where Christians are persecuted. After experiencing the **GPS Life Journey** personally, he now orchestrates **GPS Life Journey** conferences for business, professional, and religious leaders across Nigeria. Ken has significant impact in his country as he leverages Christian leadership to make a difference.

Mobilizing Atlanta

Rachel served for several years in Bosnia with university students. After returning to America to fulfill her primary role as mother to four children, she now gives leadership to a movement mobilizing people in Atlanta. Rachel facilitates **GPS Life Journey** small groups and trains and coaches others to help people find purpose in life.

Dan and Risa, business owners in Atlanta, have joined the mobilization movement in Atlanta after experiencing their personal **GPS Life Journey**. They also travel to other cities, regions and countries to help expand the mobilization movement.

And the Beat Goes On ...

These are only a handful of success stories of how individuals just like you are changing their communities and the world. There are literally hundreds of other stories and thousands more who will have such stories in the future as we continue to expand access to the **GPS Life Journey** all across America and around the world. Just recently in Nigeria, through the leadership of Pastor Ken and three other American leaders, 135 professionals discovered their God-given purposes.

What's Your Story?

Do you know God's mission for your life here on earth?

Do you understand how God has created you to fulfill that mission?

Are you actively engaged in fulfilling that mission?

Are you experiencing a sense of significance and fulfillment in carrying out your God-given mission?

Are you leaving a legacy of impact for others?

Are you making a significant difference in the Kingdom of God?

If your answer to these questions encourages you as you realize that you are truly on mission with God, share your story with others so that they can be encouraged to also fulfill their missions.

If you are not pleased with your answers to these thought provoking questions, the **GPS Life Journey** will put you on the right path to God's plan for success and significance for your life.

Remember, fulfilling your God-given mission is not about doing a lot of volunteer work and good deeds. It is about knowing and doing **"the good works which God prepared beforehand that you should walk in them."** (Ephesians 2:10)

GPS Life Journey Story...
Trained to Treat the Whole Person Now, Including Their Spirit
By Sheree Ash, MA

When asked how my husband and I met, I often humor people by sharing that he used to work with my mom. My husband frequently jokes saying, "Yes, I was the guy her mom introduced; that's not so easy to live down." On top of that introduction to my husband, our first "date" involved reading the *Purpose Driven Life* together. Well, if I'm honest, at the time that quickly shifted him into the "friend" category. Now, fast forward almost 11 years later, and he challenged me again to join him in participating in the **GPS Life Journey**. This time, quite like how my "friend" category with my husband changed, my desire to go deeper into understanding how God made me had changed too!

I am amazed at how the GPS curriculum is designed, as it has helped me hone in on my talents and abilities, and also integrate my previous life experiences. Through the GPS process, I have gained a deeper sense of appreciation and gratitude for how awesome God has "intricately" made me. I have also grown in love more with my husband, as I now see how beautifully God has placed us together to complement each other.

Today, I am more comfortable and confident in who I am. As a psychology doctoral student, I am receiving training to understand human behavior and the motivation behind it. Well, now I have my very own mission statement that helps to guide my behavior. I know who God made me to be. If there is ever a time that I don't know what to do, I simple pray, and let His Word and my mission be the lamp unto my footsteps.

Thank you **GPS Life Journey** for helping me discover my truest potential. Even more so, thank you because this will not only impact me, but forever influence the way I interact with my clients. This journey will have a rippling effect and last throughout a lifetime. I am truly honored to have taken this journey with you.

Sheree Ash lives in Atlanta, Ga where she is a Doctoral student in Clinical Medical Psychology

Five

You Are Unique for a Reason

Shape Up and Ship Out

As mentioned earlier, Christians of the world are greatly indebted to Rick Warren and his best selling book, **The Purpose Driven Life**. This book introduced the SHAPE concept. Actually, it was introduced in his previous book, **The Purpose Driven Church**.

SHAPE is an acronym for
- Spiritual Gifts
- Heart or Passions
- Abilities or Strengths
- Personality or Temperament
- Experiences

God has designed or shaped each one of us with a unique profile. While many of us share common characteristics, still we are all different. If every snowflake is created uniquely, certainly every person is unique. We have already discovered that God has a special work for each of us to do. (Ephesians 2:10) God also equips each of us with the gifts to carry out these good works He has assigned to us.

The entire Body of Christ (His Church) benefits from each of us fulfilling His purposes in His Kingdom. (Ephesians 4:12)

In reality then, each Christian is to "shape up and ship out." That is, each of us must discover and understand our God-given SHAPE and employ that in service in the Kingdom of God. God did not create us just so we could know our uniqueness, but that we might bring glory to Him using our personal profiles in ministry.

What SHAPE Are You In?

Try to identify your unique design as you examine the various components of Rick Warren's SHAPE concept below.

Spiritual Gifts

Here is a listing of Spiritual Gifts Listed in Scripture.
(I Corinthians 12, Romans 12, Ephesians 4)

Administration - The ability to organize and think strategically

Apostleship - The passion to begin new works and ministries

Discernment - The ability to test the genuineness of something or someone

Evangelism - The ability to easily share the gospel and lead others to Christ

Exhortation - The ability to encourage others with the truths of scripture

Faith - The ability to trust God in very difficult circumstances

Giving - The desire to give generously to meet needs beyond the biblical teaching of giving 10%

Healing - The faith to see people healed because of your prayers

Interpretation of Tongues - The ability to interpret what another is saying in tongues

Knowledge - The desire to learn and study resulting in an accumulation of knowledge

Leadership - The ability to inspire and cast vision for the big picture and future direction

Prophecy - The passion to speak truth in all situations with boldness and biblical clarity

Mercy - The ability to sympathize with others who have needs

Miracles - The ability to trust God to do miraculous things through your prayers and ministry

Service - The desire to serve others and meet their needs behind the scene

Shepherding - The ability to care for and mentor others using biblical principles

Teaching - The desire to search out and teach biblical truths to others

Tongues - The ability to speak in an unknown tongue or to easily learn other languages

Wisdom - The ability to know the wise thing to do in life situations

What are your primary spiritual gifts?

Heart or Passions

What things, causes, ministries, problems, or dreams excite you the most? What would you do if you could do anything? What problems would you solve in society if you could?

Abilities or Strengths

What are your greatest natural abilities? What skills have you developed because of special training? What are your greatest strengths? What things are you really good at?

Personality or Temperament

The four primary personality types are Dominate, Influence, Steadiness and Conscientiousness.

Dominate - Task-oriented, bold, likes to be in charge
Influence - People-oriented, inspirational, creative, fun-loving

Steadiness - People-oriented, serves others, does not like to be out front
Conscientiousness - Task-oriented, perfectionist, systematic

What is your primary personality type?

Experiences

What are your primary life experiences that have shaped who you are and have led you to be able to do what you do? What good and bad experiences have you had that might prepare you for special ministry in the future?

If you had difficulty identifying your SHAPE or answering any of these components concerning your personal design, the **GPS Life Journey** has accurate assessments that give you precise answers to each component of your personal profile.

As the ancient sage wisely said, ***"Know thyself."***

GPS Life Journey Story ...
I Now Understand
and Like Me
by David Anderson

I can honestly say I never understood who I was growing up. What I can tell you is I wanted to be someone else. I guess you could say I was a recovering "me" most of my life. It's not that nice things weren't said; it's just that I found it difficult to believe them.

Even after I discovered what it meant to have faith in Christ, I stumbled along the way. My salvation was radical, and I ran after God like I run after everything - with everything I have. But I still had questions. It wasn't enough to understand the fall and sin's effect on creation and ultimately how that translated to my struggles. This was more than that. I still had some kind of disconnect I could not explain.

Many years after finding Christ, and growing more than I thought I would in a lifetime, I discovered the most amazing thing. It was almost too good to be true, but as I looked more closely, it became undeniable.

I was exactly the person God created me to be and with His power I had become more of what He wanted me to become.

I had been given permission to be the very person I was, not having to be anyone else, but now able to excel at the thing I was most equipped to be - me.

In a very short time, I was shown how God loved me so much that He fashioned me to be the person He wanted. And not just that, He also allowed the circumstances of my life to further equip me to be able to glorify Him, if I was willing to be obedient to fulfill the purposes He had for me.

Now I know I am never alone and that God has a plan for me. Knowing this gives me the hope I need when times look desperate and circumstances look to be against me. More importantly than His showing me who I am is His showing me who He is.

I am grateful for the impact that the **GPS Life Journey** has had in my life. Understanding how God had designed me through the various assessments helped me love how God had made me.

David Anderson is a husband and father of six, including quadruplets. He is a certified Life Design Coach, a certified **GPS Life Journey** Facilitator & Coach, trained as a Roundtable Group Facilitator and conducts corporate retreats. He is also a Biblical counselor.

Six

Getting Your Purpose from God

Can You Hear Me Now?

For many years as a Christian leader, I was guilty of telling people "what" they should be doing as a follower of Christ without helping them to understand "how" they could do it. Most people really do want to do what they know they should be doing. They simply do not know how to do it.

I have made another discovery about Christians. We do not know how to hear from God and get His plan and direction for our lives. So when people hear a leader proclaim that they should hear and obey God, they are eager to do so but do not know how to hear from God.

We cannot live our lives in accordance with His plan and purpose for us if we do not know how to hear Him. I have had the privilege of having Dr. Henry Blackaby, author of **Experiencing God**, as a personal mentor for many years. I have heard Dr. Blackaby say numerous times, "If Christians do not know when God is speaking, they are in trouble at the heart of their Christian lives."

Even Jesus insisted that he needed direction from the Father and that He did only what He saw the Father doing around Him. (John 5:19-20) Jesus also taught us that real sheep know His voice and follow Him. (John 10:3-4)

A Personal Story

May I share just one personal story of hearing from God concerning His plan for my life?

Several years ago I thought I had arrived at the apex of my career. I was serving as Executive Pastor of a wonderful church and loving what I was doing. We had helped lead a four year process of relocating the church and building a beautiful 100 acre campus.

"This is it," I told my wife. "I have worked hard for over 30 years. We now have the privilege of serving in a great church in the paradise of Southwest Florida. I am going to slow down a bit, play more golf and enjoy the journey."

A word of warning - if you plan to take your ease and enjoy the bigger barns that you have built, don't go abroad and see what God is doing around the world. Well, that was my mistake, or I should say, that was my destiny.

I traveled to an impoverished region in the Caucasus Mountains of Southern Russia on a mission trip. While there a local pastor wanted to show me his numerous church plants in this difficult Muslim region.

Upon arriving at one of his new churches, I realized that these deeply committed Christians were meeting in a former chicken house. The chicken wire still covered the windows.

Plastic sheeting had been stretched over the wire to keep out the bitter cold Russian winter winds. Wooden benches without backs sat on the dirt floor. The ceiling was too low for me to stand up inside the building. It is a huge understatement to say it did not resemble "my church."

The Holy Spirit began to bring to me what well-known pastor and author, Bill Hybels, calls a "holy discontent." I realized that God was doing so much around the world with so little. I sensed that God was calling me to leave the comfortable ministry that I felt I deserved to fulfill a different purpose for the next stage of my life. It was a struggle to give up my plan for God's plan.

Early one Monday morning while thinking about the need to mobilize others to get involved in meaningful ministry in the Kingdom of God, I informed God, "Somebody ought to do something about this need." That was another mistake. God quickly responded, "And who would that be that should do something about this?" The answer was obvious.

That morning I knew that my journey was taking a new direction. God was speaking to me and directing me to began this new venture called Kingdom Mobilization. (www.kingmo. org)

Hearing from God may change your life. Actually, it will change your life! You may have to make adjustments, weather a crisis of belief and experience some sacrifices, but you will never regret that you followed God's plan and purpose for your life.

Yes, my golf game stinks. But the blessing of seeing hundreds of individuals living out their God-given missions is a fragrant sacrifice before the Lord.

What Is Your Experience in Hearing God?

Does God speak to you and give you direction for your life? If you cannot hear from God concerning direction for your life, how do you make crucial decisions?

I know that God definitely does speak to me and gives me direction for my life. There are two primary reasons why I know this. First, it is the record of scripture. God consistently spoke to individuals throughout scripture and gave them direction for their lives.

Second, it is the testimony or personal experience of my life. God has spoken and continues to speak to me concerning His plan for my life. I could write a large volume of illustrations on how God has spoken to me throughout my spiritual journey.

If you cannot hear and get direction from God for your life, there is only one other alternative for your decision making. You figure it out the best you can with your own abilities. Or, you have someone else help you figure it out with the best of their abilities. Either way that is the basis for humanism - the best mankind can do on their own. History reveals to us that this has not worked so well.

It Takes Time

Take the time necessary to hear from God. Hearing from God cannot be rushed. While God may seldom give you direction according to your desired schedule, He is never late. When God appears to be silent, realize that silence is also direction. When God is silent continue to do what He told you to do last and faithfully seek to learn what He is seeking to teach you during the period of silence.

Learn to Listen

If you are having difficulty hearing from God and getting direction for your life, focus your prayers on listening to God rather than talking to God. It is difficult to hear anyone else speak when you are talking.

There is a significant amount of material on hearing from God in the **GPS Life Journey.** I encourage you to take advantage of the session on *How to Get Direction from God.*

GPS Life Journey Story ...
Discipling People
to Action
by Paul Hahn

As a megachurch Education Pastor, I have been asked to consider using every resource under the sun. Don't get me wrong! I'm very grateful for those seeking to supply the church with curriculum, studies, programs, etc. After all, if it weren't for their help, I would have to spend all my time writing when God has clearly called me to spend my time with people.

So you'll understand that when I was introduced to the **GPS Life Journey**, my initial reaction was something like, "Oh, another one of these..." I had seen and used similar programs, so I wasn't that excited about GPS but I went along anyway. In my usually smug way, I already knew where it was headed and that when it was over it would be, well over!

Our group began the journey, and it wasn't long before things got unusually interesting. The facilitators leading our group got personal and objective showing us things that we had never seen before, and to my surprise, God began using me to help others in our group. Then we had that week! The week that I truly believe is unique to the **GPS Life Journey**, the week where we stop to hear from God. So I went to bed on a

Tuesday night, and when I woke up on Wednesday morning, everything had changed. The Lord made it clear to me what my mission in life was to be and the goals I needed to accomplish.

Now I'm using the **GPS Life Journey** to help others discover their Ephesians 2:10 purpose in life and I'm very excited about doing it. What GPS taught me is that people want to know their life mission but they need someone to walk them through the discovery steps in order to come to valid conclusions. That's why I'm as passionate about training facilitators as I am about new people taking the journey. And our church is benefitting greatly!

Paul Hahn is an Education Pastor at an Atlanta mega church. He serves on the staff of Woodstock Baptist Church in Northern suburban Atlanta, Ga.

Seven

Creating Margin in Life

Detour Ahead

Several years ago we were traveling from Asheville, North Carolina on I-40 back to East Tennessee where we lived at the time. It was the proverbial "dark and stormy night." We were driving late at night and it had been raining for days. Just west of Asheville we encountered a roadblock and detour sign. Those of you who are familiar with this section of interstate know that it is frequently closed because of rock slides.

We were re-routed over the mountains along narrow, extremely winding roads. We added to a "dark and stormy night" "a long and winding road." What should have been a two-hour journey turned into a stressful, four-hour nightmare.

This is how it is in life when we seek to follow God's plan for our lives. The end result is a wild, exciting adventure. But most journeys in life have detours. Even when we know His purpose and are committed to fulfilling it, we encounter detours.

I have discovered that there are three major roadblocks or detours on the journey to discovering and fulfilling God's purpose for your life. These roadblocks are a lack of time, a lack of resources, and a lack of spiritual capacity.

Success Is Seeking First Things First

Success in life is not related to your getting "caught up." It is about doing first things first. Being able to have the resources for fulfilling your mission is not merely about accumulating excess funds for ministry. It is about prioritizing the use of all the resources that God provides. Having spiritual capacity to lead and serve in meaningful ministry is not accomplished by just attending church. It is the natural overflow of pursuing an intimate relationship with Jesus Christ.

In short, you must create intentional time and financial margins and spiritual capacity in your life. Are you using your time, financial resources and spiritual capacity for maximum impact in the Kingdom of God?

Discovering and fulfilling your God-given mission is not about getting caught up or finally have excess time and money; it is about placing first things first.

Creating Time Margin

- How much time can you devote to pursuing your life purpose?

- What do you need to change in order to have time margin to pursue your mission?

- Are you willing to do first things first and leave undone other good things to pursue your life purpose? Why or why not?

Creating Financial Margin

- How much money can you devote to pursuing your life purpose?

- What do you need to change in order to have financial margin to pursue your mission?

- Are you willing to place first things first in the use of your financial resources? Why or why not?

Creating Spiritual Capacity

- How are you doing on your spiritual journey? Do you have spiritual capacity to lead or serve others?

- What do you need to change to have greater spiritual capacity?

- Are you willing to make your spiritual capacity a priority in your personal growth? Why or why not?

Detour End

Remember, you have all the time, financial resources and spiritual capacity necessary to fulfill your God-given purpose. God has given you all you need to follow His plan for your life. The key is to prioritize - make first things first.

GPS Life Journey Story ...
Giving Up My Plan for God's Plan Was a Winner, by David Parker

I lived most of my life as a nominal Christian with one foot in the church and one in the world. My plan of searching for love and happiness in all the wrong places led me to a life of desperation and addictions. It was only when I came to the end of myself and my plans and turned to God that I found peace and purpose.

I promised God that if He would give me a life of purpose I would serve Him with all my heart, soul and mind. As I diligently sought His plan for my life, God told me He was preparing me to go to the nations with His gospel. I was to eliminate all my debts, rent my house, downsize my total lifestyle and get ready to go.

During this time of preparation, God burdened my heart with a deep passion for the impoverished children in the Philippines. As I had never been there and knew little about the needs, I searched the Internet for information on the Philippines. God opened the door for me to go and I was ready, as I had obeyed Him.

My life would never be the same. A person, who before had been concerned only about himself, was now being used mightily by God to feed the poor, heal the sick, share the gospel and train disciples. All this happened because I decided to make my relationship with God my number one priority in life. I obeyed Him and adjusted my life and plan to be able to follow Him and His plan.

Jesus said that if you try to find your life in this world, you will lose it. But if you lose your life in this world you can find real life in Him and His purpose for you.

I am so grateful for the support and coaching I have received from Kingdom Mobilization and my coach, Nolen Rollins. Fulfilling my God-given purpose is rewarding and I know that God is using me to make a difference in His Kingdom.

David Parker is an electrician who works in Chicago for one half of each year and then ministers abroad for the other half. He has seen thousands accept Jesus Christ.

Eight

Just Do It !

Mission Imperative!

I loved the old TV series and the more recent movies, **Mission Impossible**. What a challenge, "Your mission, should you choose to accept it …" Those supposedly impossible missions were never declined. And now, you are issued the same challenge. God has a mission for you, should you choose to accept it. It is not a mission impossible; it is a mission imperative!

You must accept it. You must obey. "Trust and obey, for there is no other way to be happy in Jesus, but to trust and obey." (Hymn by John Sammis) Discovering and fulfilling your God-given mission is the only way to live the life of success and significance that God has planned for you. One of the best ways to experience this is participation in the **GPS Life Journey.**

The GPS Life Journey

The frequently referenced **GPS Life Journey** is not a book you can read without a coach. It is a certified facilitator-led process. In eight sessions of one to two hours you can discover your God-given purpose and develop a strategy for fulfilling that purpose. You can participate in the **GPS Life Journey** process with a one-on-one coach, in a **GPS Life Journey** blitz of two days, or in the recommended **GPS Life Journey** small group of eight sessions that usually meets for eight consecutive weeks. You can learn more about the **GPS Life Journey** at www.gpslifejourney.com.

My Personal GPS Life Journey Road Map

Should you choose to participate in the **GPS Life Journey** process, you will develop a 15 step personal road map that will guide your journey to living on purpose. You will discover ...

- My Personality Type
- My Most Important Life Experiences
- My Greatest Abilities and Skills
- My Greatest Strengths
- My Greatest Passions and Interests
- My Primary Spiritual Gifts
- My Personal Missional Core Values
- How to Get Direction from God for My Life
- My Personal Mission Statement
- Vision for the Next Stage of My Life
- Priority Goals for the Next Stage of My Life
- Personal Ministry Venues for the Next Stage of My Life
- How to Develop Time Margin for My Mission
- How to Develop Financial Margin for My Mission
- How to Develop Spiritual Capacity for My Mission

Your personal road map will help you to discover the life of significance that God has designed for you. It will keep you focused on your purpose.

Why Did God Put You Here on Earth?

God placed each of us here on earth to bring Him glory. While we tend to think everything is all about us, the Word of God is clear that everything is all about God and His glory.

The Gospel of Matthew states, "... let your light shine before others, so that they may see your good works and **give glory to your Father** who is in heaven." (Matthew 5:16) God wants you to discover and fulfill His purpose for your life. He created you for this purpose.

Just do it! Do what God created you to do ... for the glory of God!

May we help? Kingdom Mobilization exists for one sole purpose. Our mission is to help men and women discover and fulfill their God-given purposes in life. Contact us if you need help on your journey.

www.kingmo.org
www.gpslifejourney.com
nolen@kingmo.org

GPS Life Journey Story ...
I Decided to Just Do It
by Esther Harshbarger

The **GPS Life Journey** was life changing for me! I have been in church for many years but never really got engaged in significant service for Christ. Being a Christian and attending church was something I felt like I was obligated to do. I had never even asked the question, "What did God create me for?"

Then I decided to participate in the **GPS Life Journey** because so many other people in my church had taken the journey. They were constantly talking about how it made a huge difference in their lives. And it made a difference in my life as well.

At 78 years of age, I discovered that God shaped me with abilities and gifts that He wanted me to use to encourage and serve others in His Kingdom. At the beginning of the course, I was not sure that I could do anything of significance. At the end of the course, I was so motivated to get engaged in fulfilling God's purpose for my life.

Now I serve several days each week at a local retirement home loving and caring for individuals who live there and have no one else to spend time with them. They love it; I love it! One person had not been outside the four walls of his room, except for medical reasons, for two years. He was transformed into a vibrant, full-of-life individual when taken outside and engaged in meaningful conversations with new friends.

I have never been closer to God than I am now. I have never been so happy and fulfilled as I am serving God. God has me here on earth for a purpose. When you discover your God-given purpose in life, there is no stopping you - just do it!

Esther Harshbarger is a mother, grandmother, great grand-mother and friend to many. She is active in her church and other venues for loving and serving others.

Appendix A …
An Illustration of
One Church

Here are the results of the impact of the **GPS Life Journey** on one small local church that uses the **GPS Life Journey** as part of its small group curriculum.

Legacy Church, Estero, Florida

- 101 Adult Members

- 64 have participated in the **GPS Life Journey** process (64 %)

- 52 are currently engaged in fulfilling their God-given missions (81 % of GPS Grads)

Other Countries Where Legacy Church Members Will Minister in the Current Year

Belize	Canada	El Salvador
Haiti	India	Indonesia

Kenya   Nicaragua   Nigeria
Peru   Philippines   Russia
Tanzania

Local Ministry Engagement for Legacy Church Members in the Current Year

Biblical Apologetics
Biblical Counseling
Business Coaching
Life Purpose Coaching
Community Benevolence
Community Prayer
Community Service Projects
Country Club Outreach
ESL – Migrant Workers
High School Outreach
Hispanic Outreach/ Church Plant
Hope Hospice
Immokalee Foundation (Migrant Children)
Kindergarten Teacher's Aid
Bible Study Outreach
Mentoring
Marriage Enrichment
Mobilization
Nursing Homes
Outreach Projects
Political/Government
Public Schools
Scripture Distribution
Senior Adult Services
Tutoring

Note: All of these ministry involvements are outside the regular ministry programs of Legacy Church, e.g., music, worship, small groups, children, facilities, hospitality, prayer, teaching, etc.

This small church is making a huge difference in the local community and all around the world because the members have discovered and are engaged in fulfilling their God-given missions.

Appendix B …
Kingdom Mobilization Resources

(All by Nolen Rollins unless indicated otherwise)

GPS Life Journey
Discover and Fulfill Your Life Purpose
(Workbook for participation in the GPS Life Journey process)

GPS Life Journey Facilitator Manual
(Manual for facilitating the GPS Life Journey process)

GPS Life Journey: Summit Edition
(Designed for use in other countries with limited Internet access)

GPS Life Journey Facilitator Manual: Summit Edition

GPS Life Journey: Russian Edition

GPS Life Journey Facilitator Manual: Russian Edition

GPS Life Journey: Spanish Edition

GPS Life Journey Facilitator Manual: Spanish Edition

Journey by George Gundlach
How I Discovered and Engaged in My Life Purpose
(Personal GPS Life Journey story)

Mobilize by George Gundlach and Nolen Rollins
Understanding Mobilization
Starting Your Mobilization Movement
(How to Start a Mobilization Movement)

GPS Life Journey TeamWorkShop
(How to Build More Effective Teams based on Personal Profiles)

Appendix C ...
Other Mobilization
Resources

Here are other resources designed by mobilization partner organizations and movements to help you discover and fulfill your life purpose.

Embracing Purpose by Linda Slaton
(www.embracingpurpose.org)

From Success to Significance By Lloyd Reeb
(www.lloydreeb.com)

Halftime by Bob Buford
(www.halftimeinstitute.org)

Identity and Destiny by Tom and Pam Wolf
(www.identityanddestiny.com)

The 210 Project by Dan Ankenbrandt and Frank Johnson
(www.210project.com)

Appendix D ...
GPS Life Journey
Coaching

I have discovered that most people need and receive great benefit from having one-on-one coaching on their journey to discovering and fulfilling their life purposes.

Certified **GPS Life Journey** coaches are available to help you successfully navigate your journey. All GPS coaches have specific training and skills in helping people understand their unique skills and giftedness, developing specific, focused mission statements, overcoming barriers to success, and engaging in the right venues for carrying out their life purposes.

GPS Life Journey coaches have been certified by the International Coaching Certification Standards Board (ICCSB) and are members of the American College of Coaching (ACC). Additionally, all coaches are certified as **GPS Life Journey** facilitators to lead others through the **GPS Life Journey** process.

Contact Kingdom Mobilization for more information and how to engage a one-on-one coach.

www.kingmo.org
nolen@kingmo.org

Appendix E ...
The Tombstone Legacy Activity

T he purpose of the Tombstone Legacy Activity is to help you to understand and reflect on the legacy you are leaving for others.

Draw a tombstone on a piece of paper.

Put your name on the top of the tombstone as it will be listed after your death. Put your date of birth followed by tomorrow's date as the date of your death on the bottom of the tombstone.

Now, write words and/or short phrases in between your name and these dates that describe how you think you will be remembered by others, if your death were tomorrow. How would people describe you? What would people say about you?

Next, take another piece of paper and draw a second tombstone. Place your name on the top and change the date of your death on the bottom to 100 years after your birth.

Again, write in words and/or short phrases that you would like to have as your legacy after your death. What would you desire people say about you?

Compare the two tombstones. Are they similar? Are they very different? Are you satisfied with what is listed as your legacy on the first tombstone? If not, how can you change your legacy? It is never too late to change your legacy.

You may want to look at the Alfred Nobel story at the Wikipedia website to see how one person intentionally, totally changed his legacy.

Appendix F ...
Scripture Verses Related to Your Life Purpose

Jeremiah 29:11, "For I know the plans I have for you, declares the Lord, plans for welfare and not for evil, to give you a future and a hope."

Ephesians 2:10, "For we are his workmanship, created in Christ Jesus for good works, which God prepared beforehand, that we should walk in them."

John 17:4, "I glorified you on earth, having accomplished the work that you gave me to do."

Psalm 139:14, "I praise you, for I am fearfully and wonderfully made. Wonderful are your works; my soul knows it very well."

Matthew 5:16, "In the same way, let your light shine before others, so that they may see your good works and give glory to your Father who is in heaven."

Psalm 138:8, "The Lord will fulfill his purpose for me; your steadfast love, O Lord, endures forever. Do not forsake the work of your hands."

Romans 12:1-2, "I appeal to you therefore, brothers, by the mercies of God, to present your bodies as a living sacrifice, holy and acceptable to God, which is your spiritual worship. Do not be conformed to this world, but be transformed by the renewal of your mind, that by testing you may discern what is the will of God, what is good and acceptable and perfect."

Matthew 6:33, "But seek first the kingdom of God and his righteousness, and all these things will be added to you."

Ephesians 1:11, "In him we have obtained an inheritance, having been predestined according to the purpose of him who works all things according to the counsel of his will."

Psalm 57:2, "I cry out to God Most High, to God who fulfills his purpose for me."

Colossians 3:23, "Whatever you do, work heartily, as for the Lord and not for men."

2 Timothy 1:9, "Who saved us and called us to a holy calling, not because of our works but because of his own purpose and grace, which he gave us in Christ Jesus before the ages began."

Exodus 9:16, "But for this purpose I have raised you up, to show you my power, so that my name may be proclaimed in all the earth."

Proverbs 20:5, "The purpose in a man's heart is like deep water, but a man of understanding will draw it out."

Proverbs 19:21, "Many are the plans in a man's heart, but it is the LORD's purpose that prevails."

Appendix G ...
Sample Mission Statements of Former GPS Life Journey Grads

Mortgage Title Company Director
My mission is to equip and empower the people of God to understand and engage in their Kingdom work.

Non-Profit Ministry Leader
I exist to glorify God by loving my wife, giving wise counsel to my children, and deploying my abilities so that organizations prosper, and people discover and live-out their unique destiny.

Investment Advisor
My mission is to glorify God by engaging individuals and raising financial resources in support of life-changing children's and young adult related ministries.

Division Manager, Large Global Corporation
My mission is to facilitate Biblically sound studies to disciple men so they grow in Christ and impact their circles of accountability.

Accounting Firm Partner

My mission is to develop and implement Christian based after school programs in the United States that enable students to achieve their full potential and engage in God's purposes for their lives.

Doctor

My Mission is to glorify God by coaching believers to defend and teaching skeptics to accept God's Word as truth.

Business Executive

My mission is to lead a life of complete identity in Christ as evidenced by my worship, my witness and the resulting Kingdom expansion through the distribution of God's Word through the Gideons International and church planting in Southeast Asia.

Appendix H ...
GPS Life Journey
Endorsements

Bob Buford, Author and Founder of Halftime and Leadership Network

"The **GPS Life Journey** is a proven resource for mobilizing individuals for meaningful service in the Kingdom of God. Author Nolen Rollins, founder and president of Kingdom Mobilization, has been a personal friend and partner of mine for many years. The workbook demonstrates his passion for helping people discover and engage in God's purposes for their lives. It is my pleasure to recommend the **GPS Life Journey.**"

Don Gunther, Retired Vice-President Bechtel Group, Inc., Chairman, The Immokalee Foundation and Co-Founder of the Naples Wine Festival

"The **GPS Life Journey** totally changed my life. After years of success in my career I was struggling to find significance and purpose after my retirement. Participation in a **GPS Life Journey** small group and the one-on-one coaching of Nolen Rollins led me to the discovery of my life mission for the next stage of my life. I am now meaningfully engaged in leadership roles in The Immokalee Foundation and my local church.

What I am doing is making a difference in the lives of hundreds of children of the migrant farm workers in Southwest Florida. They are being prepared for a successful future in life. I highly recommend that every follower of Jesus Christ participate in the **GPS Life Journey**."

Bob Roberts, Jr., Author, Pastor Northwood Church, Dallas-Ft Worth, Texas, and Founder of GlocalNet

"The GPS Life Journey, written by my good friend Nolen Rollins, is being used effectively to mobilize thousands of individuals for meaningful service in hundreds of ministries that are changing the world. This coach/facilitator driven curriculum is helping people discover and fulfill their God-given missions in life. It is my pleasure to recommend The GPS Life Journey and the leadership of Nolen Rollins to you. I have traveled with Nolen on global trips. I have helped train leaders in his organization for mobilizing people, Kingdom Mobilization. The work he is leading is mobilizing and equipping the Church for major impact in the world."

Bill Elliff, Teaching Pastor, The Summit Church, North Little Rock, AR and Church Division Director of OneCry! A Nationwide Call for Spiritual Awakening

"I know few men who have accomplished as much for the Kingdom as Nolen Rollins. His most important accomplishments have been his uncanny ability to help others fulfill their spiritual destiny. Nolen dramatically affected my own life as friend and coach. The **GPS Life Journey** gives you access to the truths Nolen has used to help thousands find God's great journey for their lives. Every follower of Christ needs this book!"

Mark O. Wilson, Author and Senior Pastor Heyward Wesleyan Church. Heyward, WS

"Practical, down-to-earth and easy to apply, the **GPS Life Journey** by Nolen Rollins is the best Christian life-coaching guide I've ever encountered. Nolen, a wise and seasoned mentor, leads the participant on a journey of self-discovery, exploring personality, strengths, gifts and passions, which combine together for meaningful mission and vision. I highly recommend this resource to anyone who is serious about discovering their life-calling and to leaders desiring to invest purposefully in others for ministry multiplication."

About the Author

Charles Nolen Rollins is founder and President of Kingdom Mobilization, Inc. (See www.kingmo.org) He also serves as the Lead Pastor/Coach of Legacy Church in Estero, Florida and a consultant for ministries around the world. He is a certified GPS and Life Purpose Coach.

Nolen has forty years plus of experience in pastoral ministry and world missions. He has previously served on the staff of churches in Tennessee, Kentucky, Oklahoma, Georgia, Arkansas, and Florida. He has served as Executive Pastor of several large churches including First Baptist Church, Atlanta, Georgia for eight years and First Baptist Church, Naples, Florida for four years.

He is a long time student and teacher of leadership development. He has led leadership conferences and served as a leadership development consultant for several churches, denominational organizations, mission agencies, other non-profit organizations, Christian schools, and businesses.

Nolen is a graduate of the University of Tennessee, Tennessee Temple Theological Seminary, and the Southern Baptist Theological Seminary. He is listed in Who's Who in Christian Education in America and International Who's Who of Professionals.

Nolen and Clarice have been married for over 40 years and have two daughters and seven grandchildren. They reside in Estero, Florida.